Something To Cry About

First Printing: 2019

Paperback ISBN: 978-1-7330279-1-5

Cover art by Jeanne Wilkinson.
Designed and edited by C. M. Tollefson

Cathexis Northwest Press

cathexisnorthwestpress.com

Something To Cry About

by

Robert T. Krantz

Cathexis Northwest Press

Dedicated to the misfit, the alien,
and the lonely.

Table of Contents

Whitman in Canada

Our dying didn't
matter to many,
silence of our song
becoming a palette
for adolescent
chortles and chants
for more or less.
I remember our first kiss
in Canada that grew like
cities on plains—
spears of wheat,
new roots earth-desperate
and starving.
For once, nothing
arose from the past,
no green tides
to pull our moods
over these naked swells
of blue sage and heather—
clear-eyed moon
speaking bold yesses
to its own hovering.
In the evening,
you lounge on the settee
of the hotel portico,
thinking of undergraduate
cigarettes and Niagara Falls.
I read Whitman,
last page to first—
beginning with death,
ending in light.

Caesura

Two-hundred miles
of spanning Ontario plains
can't help us now,
Stratford standing
halfway between
Detroit and The Falls—
moonlit intermission
of Beaujolais and brie.
We argue like lovers—
in silence,
iambs sliced in two,

moats of blank verse
spill out over burning rivers,
deep gorges
of misunderstanding.
Midsummer, I grasp your myth,
clutch your magic,
and you, whisper my folly.
We find no middling words
to bridge this
undiscovered country,
no kisses,
no mumbled apologies . . .
I think of you often—
your aria never stops
praying for rest.

Pearl

I remember the wheat fields
of Iowa and the photograph
of you I took with me,
and how neither ever ended—
edges splayed with mysterious horizons
and miraculous loaves.
We ate and loved
much in that decade,
collided with stars,
authored myths
and stuffed our age-spotted hands
into denim pockets,
watching the children
move from our sides
as is their nature.
Tonight the harvest moon
is full and I wait for its tides
to pull something living
out of these bluish seas.
The half shells we find on beaches
were once a thing joined together,
breathing, and grinding
new pearls into place.

Row

I hate the way
the moon pulls you
like an ocean
towards herself,
bends you
into tropical depressions—
there are fugues
played on flutes
on beaches
and bonfires
that burn scribbled notes
I couldn't send you
I hear their crackling ashes snap
see them rise like fireflies
then extinguish ...
some nights come full circle
the rim of a drum beating
a cadence that keeps
my enslaved shoulders pulling
away from safe shores
and faint fires now burning
on your foreign sands

Daedalus

You asked if the rabbit
knows about the hawk
      (Is it better to know?)
that tied your mind
with a frayed wire,
and you cried and cried.
How could God be so cruel?
I wanted to answer
that life can be brutal—
a bloodied knuckled bully
at the end of an alley—
but I didn't want to worry
you with all my falcons, eagles
and owls, and every man's
own waxed wings.

      That night you dreamt
      of skinless mice,
      hearts pounding
      in your tiny hand,
      and I knew you knew
      what I didn't say,
      and I did not ask
if you squeezed them.

To Cordelia

The letters I wrote
in invisible ink
asked for more
than possible,
held over the flames
of midnight candles,
now curl at edges of
dead seas, black
and salty from
the sweat of hard labor . . .
So what if on Sundays
I play football
(the persnickety game)
with the fellas,
tossing fate
this way and that
while your silence
looms over the pitch
like a holy spirit?
We have since built
stone hovels,
makeshift and gray,
to house onyx cats
and grave elixirs.
I met a woman in college
named Marcy,
the glass menagerie type,
with spectacles and
a nasty way of saying
I love you—

and all the other things
a woman could say,
her whispers faint
like a broken child's.
Now I pray to the power
that animates the seed
I pray to dirt and light
I pray
and pray

Self-Defense, I Swear

It's not bad that the pit bull runs free
through the strip mall parking lot
there's a wire around her muzzle
which comforts me plenty
here's the man who's lost the tramp
here girl, here girl
she doesn't bite
she just gets excited
the man grabs her collar,
jerks her away from my crotch
why the zip tie?
well, she bit once
but it wasn't like you're thinking
oh, that's good
I was thinking the worst
everyone does
they run away together ...
the neighborhood's changed
over the past three years
more rust, less foliage
more noise--car horns, garbage cans,
street cleaners, sirens
the pharmacy is a mirage still,
wavering two-hundred yards away
makes me wish I'd Uber-ed
the mile and a quarter
but they get pissed
when you do that
even if you tip well
I watch a sheriff
pull over a Buick,

carefully inch
along the side of the car,
hand on holster...
it is April and the squirrel fills
his mouth with colorless grass
scurries up a tree,
to his incomplete nest
at home, I turn on Bob Marley
and wonder if he drove a Buick

Relief

Rain doesn't bother us
as it did at Houghton,
where we stood in fat mud
and built makeshift vows
with flame and stake,
ferreted out weed
and stone before taking
inevitable steps
into mercurial waters.
I color your eyes black
and shape your lips
into a smile, every drag
of cigarette turns the trodden arc
into an O—"I'm not a doll,"
you say. Once again we stand
at our slate palette, fluff our brushes,
and splash painted questions
against the Braille night sky.
In Autumn, the red maples burn
like tongues of fire, speak wise words
to the middle-aged and weary.
You write gauzy ink goodbyes
in sunken letters
chiseled like an epitaph
into my granite heart.

Doll

When we argue,
your porcelain mouth
moves like a puppet,
speaks waves of riddles
and madness, glassy blue eyes
sparking flint to fire.
I've cobbled this January mask
to look both ways
toward your scarecrow hair
and back at spires of firs
and black lakes.
Still, you prick me
with bone-white fingers
saying, "here!"
and "hear!"
After, while you are sleeping
I search for threads,
loose and frayed
at your wrists and toes,
shoulders and waist,
cords that coil
like silk strands.
Our masters pull us
loose like teeth,
leave us face-up and stuck
between open and closed—
your ink eyelashes
smudge pretty notes on flitting lids

Wreck

A sunken ship is an eerie
thing, these fish have no language
to describe its descent–this vessel had one job, to float

I swim in a wordless cloud behind the rusted rudder
no new lexicon will resurrect this hulk
but I feel the vague words,

opaque in spheres above my head,
watch them bubble
to their strange surfaces

the acts we do in cars,
the screams and ecstasies,
spill out onto streets and highways

like deer blood and bone
combing restless children's hair,
you are the tooth of the pick

that lifts the louse
crying won't help–
the spirit had no ears to hear

these earthly songs
a salt mouth full of sea
we are all drowning

Breathe

We race storm
clouds east
past Chelsea
and Dexter,
small places
where stray dogs
in strange markings
turf tangle
under starless skies.
Perhaps better to stop,
toss our grizzled bones
to street corners,
rent rooms over
a bar on Main Street
or turn into the night,
face-first with apostle courage.
Canvas of pounding rain,
black like oil against
our best layers and
the gray sky whispers
vague proverbs.
I take to wandering,
drag my feet through ashes
with hungry prayers
on my lips
that move like tides
between my body
and yours.

Call

This long summer night
I hike low meadows
now patched with white wildflowers,
searching for the forgotten stone
of a fatherless friend, long dead
from cirrhosis or shame.
I wish it were winter
and yearn for more hours
with ashen clouds,
squalls stinging face,
biting arms
and chest through coat.
I crave a deeper darkness—
to slip into ice-masked pools,
pitiless and black,
meet myself faceless;
gently freezing
into the loss of you.
the Hail Mary's,
the Our Father's,
the Glory Be's
won't lift the soot
from this pit
I've clawed out,
harrowed with fists in fits.
at the edge
of a windswept forest,

I call
Father,
Jesus, John,
embrace the echoed stillness—

An elm's twin seed
drifts earthbound,
silently swayed
by the hand of God.

Vein

The statue of Luke
sinks into ground,
mossy hand
blessing the living
and the dead.

The purple crocus blooms
to a chord
of sacred silence:
your prayer—
etched in hollow bones

your prayer—
marrow of the oak
your prayer—
inscribed on locust leaf,
your naked thoughts

dance like vertigo
before me,
a resurrection of yesses
breathed into the
capillaries of my granite eyes

Seed

And then I returned
to ash, alone
near my woman's
breathing body,
soft hands
spreading me wild,
saying here,
and here,
and here.
Moss grows green
beneath the locust,
a palette of silence
for the dropping bud
and drunken bee.
It is a time
for falling peaches
and the salmon moon.
I empty my hands
of all that is not mine
to harvest.

Load

The bachelors
in the laundromat
spill their words
like bleach
on black clothes,
speak of condos
and alimonies--
thick humidities turning.
I watch damp thoughts tumble
and wish for aridity,
a place where exposure
chaps thirsty lips
and breathes
restless poems
into my blues and grays.
Soon this summer rain
will end, volume of water
striking pavement
will knob itself silent.
The cash machine,
against the flecked wall,
reminds me to change.

Dirt

A new flower tattoo
for each disappointment
I see your garden blossom
from shoulder to sleeve
I've always loved your hands
strong and laboring
buried in the dirt of it all

Anchor

We consider the moon
personally, halving the miles
between it and us
through scoped portholes

and bedtime prayers.
So what if we can't discern
the Fates from the Furies
even as they tug our sheets

while we dream electric dreams.
We all have dings and dents
where we want them least,
and launch these iron anchors

into tempestuous waters—
currents that sweep
us off the edge
of the world,

toward the end
of all things.

After

You stood at the corner
of the Mobil station,
pay phone receiver
gripped in hand.
I remember your words
like sharp yesterdays,
digging my claws
into those rocky cliffs.
Now we fly like crows
through autumn skies
wings beating quick rhythms,
dire divings
into each other's
bodies and breath.

Did you notice
the moon's breeze
that wrapped us
in whispers
while we floated above
low meadows,
feel them touch
your softer parts?
I search for where the wind begins
and plan to meet you there.

Puppets on Pegs

Our grave owl
eyes can't pierce
the pitch of
another speechless
night where everything
feels like falling
stone gray
and coarse feathered,
eyes fixed
and always looking down—
the spiders crawl
our sleeping throats,
recover phantom letters
of words unspoken—
in your inside, inside voice
you ask if I love you
and I turn my head
and turn my head
and turn my head
to see you
when I say
I will.

Acknowledgements

"Whitman in Canada," "Caesura," "Relief," and "Doll" were originally published by Cathexis Northwest Press

"Daedalus" was originally published by High Shelf Press

"Pearl" was originally published by Antiphon & Grasslimb

"Seed" was originally published by Grasslimb

"Row" was originally published by Antiphon

"Wreck" was originally published by Gargoyle

"Call" and "Vein" were originally published by The Faithful Creative

"Dirt" was originally published by The Inflectionist Review

Cathexis Northwest Press

CPSIA information can be obtained
at www.ICGtesting.com
Printed in the USA
LVHW081223040919
629883LV00028B/3513/P